Strangers Among Strangers

Through The Eyes of a Decorated Armed Forces Veteran

Author, A.J. Thompson

Manager, Cheryl A. Thompson

Editors
A.J. Thompson
Cheryl A. Thompson
Shawanna C. Thompson
Deja D. Lawson

Introduction

As time passes, I gain a better and deeper understanding of what veterans go through upon and after exiting from their tour of duty from the military and finally coming home to their families and friends.

I have also learned what the family members, of both Armed Forces Veterans and Active Duty Service people alike, have had to survive and live through as well.

I have learned all of this from what I've gone through as a U.S. Armed Forces Veteran, from the many things I still deal with and go through, and most importantly, from what my family and friends have gone through and continue to go through resulting from my return to the fold.

For the most part, my family, like the families of so many other Vets and Active Duty people, still go through the trauma of not recognizing who their Veteran or Active Duty person has become. It is mostly due to the lack of understanding that they are now, for the most part, strangers. This is something that I have come to understand so clearly, so delicately, so undeniably and so devastatingly.

Believe me, this I know and understand, and has become both my help and my life: the "It" is trauma, rejection, suspicion, insecurities, paranoia, insomnia, received and perceived threats, and abandonment. It is that most of us Veterans and Active Duty people have become strangers among our families and friends, and they have become strangers to us as well.

Upon our return home, we are not the same people who left home to serve our country. We have become strangers because we've been trained and conditioned to a higher standard, a higher alertness, and a higher awareness than most.

We are strangers because we've evolved from that boy or girl that families and friends once knew before we became a force to be reckoned with.

That is terrifying to our families and friends and to people who don't even know us. That is because we are now different from almost everyone else, and there's really no denying that.

That makes us strangers almost everywhere we go, except on military installations, Veterans Administration Hospitals, Veterans of Foreign Wars (VFW), Disabled American Veterans (DAV), American Legions posts, homeless shelters, private military, and some churches, where our new unspoken family now meet. These now are really the only places where our hearts can somehow find solace as home among other Veterans, Active Duty people, and families who all go through the same things.

What we now share with our birth families is that we have become strangers to each other. By this time, there are rarely any old friends. Those who once were friends have diminished to being only acquaintances, as we have also become to them.

Because of that, America's people, which is to include our own families, constantly knowingly and unknowingly do hurtful and damaging things to their Armed Forces Veterans.

Our own people and our own families and friends talk negatively about us. They call us crazy and even tell others that the military has made us crazy, From our perspective, what the U.S. Military Forces has done is fine-tuned, sharpened, and maximized the powers of who we are.

Chapter 1:
Stop Hurting Us!

Most Americans support their U.S. Forces Service people in times of national conflict. Though once we have put our lives on the line in securing and safeguarding our Country and her People, we are then often referred to as murders and monsters; as cold, vicious, heartless, and as sinners who could never be forgiven.

This would repeatedly be our reward and treatment by those same folks who supported us when threats were on their lives, way of life, and on ours at the times when we were needed to do what only we could do.

Mind you, all of this takes place shortly after giving some of us a public hero's welcome home. That is so confusing and so heart-piercing.

Then, our own Homeland (one's own home country/residency) families and friends con us, steal from us, lie on us, lie to us, fight us, and provoke us to violence; all the while, having no idea what we are capable of, nor the amount of positive strength and energy that it takes for us to maintain.

This is because of their learned behavior. They are subliminally alerted from within themselves that the person standing in front of them, who is supposed to be you, is not you, but a stranger whom they have never met, and has somehow gotten into their perimeter (particular space/ area).

That then creates an instant, insecure, and hostile environment followed by a series of mental and spiritual attacks and assaults, and often physical attacks against the active Service Member or Veteran.

This environment is created by our families, and friends, as well as by other Homeland people (people who have the home country/residency as ours), by the people we served, and still serve, to keep safe and protected with every aspect of our lives, and by people who should be our friendlies (friendly forces toward us).

That then leads to certain physical attacks, assaults, separation, isolation, distrust, reclusion, distancing, detachments, disassociation, and divorce against their Veteran and Armed Forces family members and friends.

By now, you're probably thinking, "not me", "not my family", and "not my friends." Or, maybe you're thinking that you know you are not that kind of friend, and or that you have never treated any Active Duty person or Veteran that way.

Well, you could be suffering from denial or just lying to yourself. It is a common thing among most people. Or maybe you're thinking, "that is exactly how it is", and maybe how prior to reading my book, you could have been totally unaware of the way you behave toward people who are different, seem different, and have different standards and values. These are people who your mind register as strangers.

You probably never realized the affects and effects of "stranger-ism". You probably never openly thought of or referred to your Active Duty or Veteran Armed Forces husband, wife, sister, brother, aunt, uncle, son, daughter, mother or father as strangers among you. Or had you?

Maybe you thought it, but it seemed wrong to say it, but you felt it and thought it. Or maybe it seemed that it couldn't or shouldn't be true, but everything about them seemed very strange in your spirit and in your thoughts.

There may have been times when you even came close to saying the word "stranger", but you quenched it for fear or for the uneasiness of what others might think of you if you spoke it out loud; that the one who is supposed to be your veteran family member, is actually now a "stranger" to you.

Stranger! Now that explains so much! Because family and friends can't hurt, do, and say harmful things like that, and abandon their own family members and friends.

It is because these are the people who they love and care for. They just can't do it. Because their love and compassion for them runs too deep and too strong. For those reasons, they just couldn't do them that way.

However, people can, and will hurt strangers without much of a problem at all. Believe me when I tell you this, people can hurt strangers by themselves as a single individual, and people can hurt strangers collectively, conspicuously, and unscrupulously.

People, both knowingly and unknowingly, hurt strangers on a regular basis and in many different ways: spiritually, mentally, physically, financially, verbally, silently, and electronically.

Through both actions and lack of actions, America hurts our Veterans and Active Duty Services People in so many ways. On many, many occasions people hurt U.S. Military people, all while telling them "thank you for your service to our Country".

That is because everyday people don't understand what we've gone through, what we've done, or who and what we are. Therefore, they don't know how to relate to the new us. In most cases, and for the same reasons, nor do we know how to relate to non-military people and matters either.

We hurt our Armed Forces Veterans in the way we celebrate them upon their return home. Let me explain. We have big family gatherings, cookouts, parades and ceremonies one day, maybe even a few, but once we're home, most of our families then solidly reject us.

It is because to them, we've become total strangers; like someone they have met, yet do not know. Someone who is not the person they once knew nor the person they were expecting.

So, they subliminally, spiritually, and mentally reject us to protect themselves. Each person's mental and spiritual alarm system alerts them to what and who they don't understand as a preconceived threat.

When that happens, because we are geared by God to live, we act accordingly to the perceived threat to sustain ourselves. So, the way people behave is not abnormal, just misguided and misperceived.

Again, this is because almost nothing about your Veteran and Active Duty family member or friend is the same as it was before they initially went into the military.

It is impossible for them to have remained the same, just as that veteran's family members and friends have grew and changed during that time, too.

We hurt our Armed Forces People in the way we celebrate they're coming home with big loud noises. They have not had time to process and adjust to the sounds and noises of peacetime (time of space with the absence/free of war, battle and conflict) from those of missions and battles. Most people don't realize it, but it really takes a lot for us veterans to hold it together during times such as those.

Those types of ceremonies often trigger in us an ongoing alert and readiness, along with an uneasiness, to react to perceived conflict which often causes us to fall into a mode of awaiting confirmation of orders to return fire (formal military authorization to engage)

It is the most horrifying feeling for us Armed Forces Veterans and Active Duty People to try to discern which sounds represent a threat from what don't, and to try to discern for which purpose the sounds and noises were made while maintaining a state of readiness to defend and protect everyone else without concern for ourselves.

Things are different for us when these circumstances are presented at secured military installations or on battlefields where we know what all the sounds are, and we are conditioned in instantaneous reactions accordingly.

What civilians attempt to do for us, in good gesture, is to most of us, like being in the jungle in the middle of the city. You know; where everything is out of place and nothing is as it should be.

In other words, it creates an atmosphere where for most Armed Forces Veterans and Active duty, especially those who have been in action and has been wounded, that becomes difficult to distinguish real from unreal, celebration from strike or attack, where we came from, and where we are.

There isn't much that gives the true reading as familiar. So, we walk around on silent, higher alert readiness, and on 24-hour duty to guard and protect our surroundings and everyone in it. Because that is what we have been irreversibly forever trained to do.

This is not something you can just flip a switch and turn on and off. An all clear sound, sign, or cease fire is required in most cases.

People hurt our Veterans when they present them with big welcome home "hire the Vets first" promotions. Most times, when Vets go out to apply for those jobs, we are turned away, deceived and lied to. This is mostly because of the silent perceived threat that we as Vets seemingly pose against them; a threat that can't be further from the truth.

There are many businesses that advertise that they hire Vets first, yet when we apply, they don't. They often tell us that the position has been filled. We've been trained to follow up, and when we do, the position usually has not been filled, or the position had never existed in the first place. At other times, those positions were filled some time later.

There is just so much fake "we hire our Vet's first" and "we hire our heroes" advertisement used simply for the sake of more sales. They have no interest or concern for Veterans and our heroes whatsoever. Then those heroes, those U.S. Armed Forces Veterans, are left in the undesirable and undeserving position of needing to apply for unemployment benefits to be able to provide for themselves and their families. Some way to honor our heroes, huh?

Is that how the people who have freely dedicated their lives to our Nation's defense, done things that can often never be uttered in that defense should be treated? Is that how America's heroes should be treated? The answer is an astounding No, but that is how most people treat "strangers".

These attacks are too often far worse than the wounds of combat battles. Those attacks cause us to become sick in many ways: mentally, spiritually, physically, and tactically. It is the pains of rejection, abandonment, shame, disgust, and distrust that leaves us depleted and displaced.

We Veterans are then left with undecipherable pains and wounds and are pushed to an unwarranted position of having to apply for VA benefits, food stamps and housing assistance, too. It is as though we are penalized for having been on active duty, and for having served our Country and Country Persons (people having the same home country/residency as ours) as well.

For most U.S. Military Veterans, there are longer waiting periods than for most non-military, which causes us Vets and our families even greater hardship.

Then there are the utilities companies that are just too tough in their dealings with Veterans. They have no consideration for our situations and treat us as harshly as they do with most of their non-veteran and non-military customers who don't pay their bills. WE ARE NOT THEM!

Lenders often rip us off with higher interest rates. These are a series of ongoing attacks, assaults, and hurtful things by our own Country persons (people having the same home country/residency as ours) against the men and women who serve our country.

Chapter 2:
Strangers Among Strangers

Our families, whom we allow access to our finances when we are away so that they can live comfortably and without worry, often waste, misuse, and abuse our monies and resources to the point that none remain for the Veterans and Active Duty family .

Our spouses, because of distance and loneliness, often spend up all our resources and money in a love affair while we are away. Often, it is with a best friend or another family member. This affair often leads to having children that the veteran knows is not his, but for the sake of everyone else, he pretends that he doesn't know.

For most of us Veterans, at that time, it seems to be the most safe, honorable and wisest thing to do for everyone, especially for the child born from it and who is totally innocent.

All of this is done while trying to put some understanding to it and some acceptable justification and excuse for the spouse, the friend, and for the family members, too.

Too often, because we don't say anything, people think we don't know what is going on, or what has happened. Though what's happening is that we are trying, with all our being and training, to maintain discipline.

We are then assessing the situation and threats, if any, and devising a set of strategies to achieve a positive resolution. Mostly though, we are trying to protect those we love at all costs.

All these types of things make Armed Forces Veterans and Active Duty People begin to seem numb, cold, and distant. There are occasions when we get lost during the attacks and misunderstandings of "stranger-ism", abandonment and deception, and are simply trying to find our bearings.

We're trying to get a grasp on what is going on around us, on what is and what isn't, on what is deliberate and what is not, but mainly, on what action is best for all, usually apart from ourselves.

Often, these are times when we are adapting. We really don't waste a lot of time on pain and sorrow until far later in life.

Instead, we spend our time strategizing and implementing plan after plan to make it better, or to find another way to do it a better way.

Our thought processes are always to transform what will not work into what will and does work. We are even trained and conditioned to forgive our families, friends and countrymen (people having the same home country/residency as ours). That's what enables us to go on, though it doesn't take away the pain; at least not all the time.

My current wife has concluded and says that I will always be military. After all this time, she says I continue to behave like an Armed Forces Service Person. She says that I still act like military and still addresses situations in a concise military manner. I personally don't think that it is a bad thing.

She says that I treat our children and grandchildren like they are in the military and that deep thinking is required in everything. She goes on to say that it's not a bad thing- just so very different. I must confess: I am different.

I also confess that the military helped to make me different. Personally, I like being different. Because of that, most people don't like that I am different even though they say that they do. This is especially true for people who have not set standards for themselves. To them, my comrades and I are like Enemies of the State (as people who have be accused of crimes such as treason against one's own country and government), and most of them do their best to treat us that way.

People who do have set standards, but who tend to oppress others, are intimidated by me and by other people like me. That is because their own spirits alert them that we are still part of the United States Armed Forces, and we are still in defense mode of our Nation and of her people; regardless of the clothing we now wear throughout the various communities in which we now live.

We seem to be forever " Strangers among Strangers".

We seem like strangers; however, we are not. We are simply armed with a higher degree of care, knowledge, skills, power, courage, accomplishment, and tenacity than most. If people would get to know us, they'd find out that all of us are all in their favor and in the favor of our Country.

Chapter 3:
Never Be The Same

I want you to understand that no person can do what our Active Duty and Veteran Armed Forces People do and have done in the name of God and Country, and in the name of National Security then remain the same person they once were.

The individuals we grew up as could not have done what was needed to be done in defense of our Country. The people that we have become could and would defend when and if necessary.

Some veterans become what some people would call violent; though they are only doing what they've been trained and conditioned to do under hostile fire and attack.

Because of series of long bomb-like physical and subliminal attacks and assaults, both actual and perceived, against many Veterans and Active Duty persons, we often arrive at place of not being able to recognize friendly forces (people and forces that are supposed to be on our side, our allies, and a friend toward us) from our foes (absolute enemies).

This is far too often due to the Armed Forces Service person's family members and friends' inability to mentally, spiritually, physically and academically recognize and confirm; nor emotionally, mentally, spiritually, and physically acknowledge and accept and connect with the Service Person.

For example, "Joel" or "Susie" isn't the same person that left to go into the military. Because of that, now Joel or Susie's family and friends are not friendly but are quite hostile and distant.

The Armed Forces husband or wife that left home does not have the same touch, hug, or kiss as they once had when they return home.

Sometimes, these details are not fully detected by friends and family during leave of duty visits, or it is just not clear then, but still suspicious. However, it becomes clearly and silently alarming to our family and friends once we are home to stay.

Even though the touches, hugs, and kisses for a short time may appear to be the same, the feel and things and experiences that you have in common that would allow you to connect with another is now gone. For now, both the Armed Forces person and their family and friends, are merely attempting to co-exist as strangers among strangers with such hesitancy and guardedness, that Armed Forces person suffer a new

wound from the emptiness and subliminal rejection of their civilian spouse, family, and friends.
Their civilian spouse is violated by a stranger with the same name with an image of her spouse who went into the military but is now seemingly not them.

Even the dog senses that the Armed Forces person have changed. However, the dog sense with deeper understanding, deeper compassion, and deeper acceptance than most people do.

What happens next is that many Armed Forces Active duty and Veteran Services People retreat and sometimes retaliate. Many of us spend our lives in retreat for what we believe is the safety of everyone else.

We are then recalled to and remain in what can be referred to as a mode to protect and serve our country continually and effortlessly. Even when almost everything and everyone in the country seems to have abandoned us, we still consider our family, friends and our country persons (people having the same home country/residency as ours) first. That leaves many Veterans living in exile smack dab in the middle of everyone else.

Many young veterans become so discombobulated in this process of strangers among strangers that they end up going back to the battlefield occupation, on military missions, and black operations because they will have become the safest, most stable, and most familiar places that they now know and are comfortable. We become most comfortable, most calm, and in control in dangerous places facing our Nation's known enemies.

Understand that this is the same place where all Armed Forces People, at first, longed to come home from, to return to their families, friends and our own country persons (people having the same home country/residency as ours).

Though by this point, the places they once longed to be away from will have become their new home, the places they understand and relate to, and the places that are presumed to understand them. These are the places where great enemies reek (at their worse and most hostile and deadly state), where there is no confusion, or questions of who is who.

Those places will have become a place of solitude in that the enemies' hostile fire is far less painful and less damaging against most Armed Forces Services People than those assaults and attacks by their own home, family, and friends, both aware and unaware. Either way, it brings upon us great pain and discomfort.

Attacks like those upon us by the people we love and stand in defense of are things that systematically disarm and kill Armed Forces People in ways that nothing else can. This also leaves far too many American Armed Forces Active Duty and Veteran

People longing for the cradle of families and friends that are no more. He or she then settles on dying among recognizable enemies as opposed to the tumultuous suffering of trying to live as a stranger amidst their families, friends, and fellow Americans by whom they are gravely misunderstood.

American Armed Forces People, both Active Duty and Veterans alike, conclude to do that in behalf of and in defense of those strangers who they remember as family and friends, and who no longer see them that way.

The Armed Forces person will have tried to live among them again, and again, but could not, due to the overwhelmingly constant array of misplaced friendly hostile fire (people who are supposed to be friends and, on our side, attacking and treating us with the utter hostility of mortal enemies) and assaults against them by those who they care for and fight for.

All veterans become sick, at least, that's what it's being called. Though what it is happening is suffer from the wounds of sadness, loneliness from the assaults and attacks of rejection, abandonment, and being unloved and friendless.

Those attacks and assaults then initiate the processes that begin to break down a person's vital organs. It stems from a series of blows to one's mental, spiritual, academic, and physical being. Then without the attention needed to recover, a person's health begins to grow worse over time.

Too often, we Armed Forces Active Duty and Veteran People don't realize that we have changed and that our families and friends have also. We don't realize that we have become strangers among strangers. Therefore, we don't understand how to recover.

Many of us old Veterans hang around at Veterans Administration Hospitals indirectly trying to get a fix of some sort of family and moral support. You see, Veterans Administration Hospitals and the other Veterans Organizations have now covertly become the closest remaining thing to genuine family and friends. That is the real medicine if you ask me.

This seems to be the only place that we can relax and let down our guards from the hostile friendly fires and attacks by our stranger families and friends who we are among.

We are well conditioned on many different levels, for many different purposes, in the art of national security and keeping America safe, but as for indifferences, rejection, abandonment, distancing and the change of family, not so much.

Chapter 4:
Murdered On American Soil

There is another major blow to us U.S. Armed Forces Active Duty and Veterans alike. It is the heaviness of murder and mayhem sweeping across America by Americans against other Americans, against their own families and friends, and the people they most likely played with and grew up with.

Armed Forces Service People return to the Homeland, and people are killing one another right here in The United States of America. This is the place that we rendered service with one of our main purposes of keeping peace within the Homeland and to defend America and Americans against all terrorists, both foreign and domestic, but here we are doing it to ourselves.

We have a lot of immoral idiots right here on American soil that are murdering, maiming, oppressing and terrorizing one another. They are doing everything we've put our whole lives on the line for to prevent from happening by other countries and non-Americans.

That is so saddening for Armed Forces People, especially for us Veterans. It makes most of us feel like what we did was all a waste of time and life and had no real purpose.

It brings tears to my eyes, and to the eyes of many others, as we hear of the too often murders riddling U.S. communities. It also happens when we hear of corrupt government practices, corrupt officials, corrupt religious leaders, and of tyranny in our own Country, especially when it is practiced by those who are supposed to look out for and safeguard the American People.

It is very difficult for Armed Forces Veterans, like me, to stand by and do nothing. We are trained to take action against tyranny on the behalf of the American people and follow through with it until it is accomplished.

That is just not the way we have been molded and shaped. We remain true to the core even as we live as strangers among strangers.

Many of our Armed Forces People are violently murdered on Homeland(our own country and place residency which we serve and defend) streets by those who are supposed to be fellow Homeland people (people having the same home country/residency as ours, and who we serve, defend and protect). This is after they have served, survived, and defied all the odds of combat and often during multiple tours of duty.

Our own people destroy our own war machines that America's enemies were unable to destroy, and all by senseless Americans for senseless reasons, or for no reasons at all.

As Armed Forces Service People, we ought to be safe within our Homeland (our home country/residency and among the people and place that we serve, defend and protect) and among our own people that we've served and defended to keep safe, but it has not been that way.

Lance Corporal Robert Crutchfield survived 14 months of hostile enemy fire and attacks in Iraq as he fought there alongside our comrades defending America's way of life and to prevent war on the Homeland. When the 21-year-old Lance Corporal returned to his hometown for Christmas, he was shot in the neck, robbed, and murdered at a bus stop in Cleveland, Ohio by an American civilian (a citizen and resident of the same United States in which he served, defended and protected).

This Defender of our Homeland was murdered in a horrific attack among these strangers who should have been friendlies. In my opinion, had Lance Corporal Crutchfield known he was among strangers, given Lance Corporal Crutchfield's Marine Corps training, he would not have been murdered by them. Instead, they would have been restrained or killed by the Corporal in self-defense.

There are literally hundreds, if not thousands, of U.S. Active Duty and Veteran Troops (Military People) murdered each year on the home front (within the borders of their own country and residency) in isolated crimes among strangers of the Homeland for various unwarranted reasons.

Sometimes, the murders are at the hands of spouses who wanted to move on but felt trapped or just wanted to retain their military spouse's military benefits, but without their military spouse.

Some people set up murder by cop scenarios often claiming fear for their lives. This is all happening while they commit every possible act they can think of to provoke their spouses who are or were Armed Forces Military into a combative attack mode. You just don't do that if you are fearful for your life.

Because we Armed Forces persons are indeed strangers among strangers, usually, local law enforcement, and nearly anyone else, fall for those deceptive acts and become allies with whomever is against the now estranged Armed Forces Services Person; even though their only wrong was that they returned home changed while the spouse also changed.

In many poor and Black Communities, Armed Forces Active Duty and Veteran persons are murdered simply out of envy and jealousy. They are now different and have higher standards, morals, as well as an earned sense of accomplishment and sense of belonging. In short, they have become great men and women, and if they were already great, they returned even greater. This has made them strangers out-numbered by other strangers who had changed also, or who are strangers because they had not changed at all.

People who were in a gang or who was headed in that direction, went into the military. They became groomed and conditioned to a higher calling and will return home as strangers who usually will not return to a lower standard of life. Yet, they do not realize that they are now strangers. They are now envied, and even intimidating to the thought process of some.

For those reasons, those Armed Forces heroes are too often murdered by strangers that they thought were friends. Our new way of life and new character seems to pose a threat to these strangers and cowards who share no appreciation for those Armed Forces heroes and for what they have done to safeguard and secure America.

Chapter 5:
It's Your Life or Mine

There are astounding numbers of suicides among U.S. Armed Forces Active Duty and Veteran People. There are several reasons for these suicides. Among the greatest of them is that they are treated as strangers by those whom they love and care for most.

They are met with long strands of rejection, hate, dismay, deception, and betrayal, which explodes in the core of their hearts and causes them overwhelming pain and heartache. It becomes easier for them to take their own lives than to retaliate against those they are sworn to protect, or to live under such heinous attacks.

Some commit suicide because it is unbearable to live with the constant memories, reminders, nightmares, and trauma of the deeds they've done in defense of our Country, and too often, those deeds were induced by corrupt and greedy politicians with corrupt political agendas through fraudulent and misleading intelligence information.

Through that, many innocent lives were taken under those misguided threats of National Security. In reality, there were none, only selfish greed at the expense of the lives of so many. The thoughts of that alone is far more than just a notion.

Then, there are those Armed Forces People who cannot adapt to civilian life because of the unrest due to the heightened awareness of their minds and the insensitivity of the mind of the strangers which they are among.

Even though their bodies have returned the same to the Homeland, their minds and souls are still engaged in missions and conflicts of war.

The Armed Forces person cannot discern friendly forces from hostile forces mainly because they are among strangers who are supposed to be friendly forces, but behave against them in hostility, deceit, and distrust.

The Armed Forces person then does what he has been trained to do: sacrifice his own life to protect and defend innocent Americans, even from themselves. If you don't understand that, all you can see is some fool who killed himself, or that they he was crazy. Others never conceive that he did it to protect you from his capabilities as a war machine. We are commissioned to eliminate all threats against America and against American people; that includes any President of the United States, along with our American Flag, "Old Glory", without waiver and without reservations.

Others commit suicide because they've arrived at a place where the sounds and scenes of duty, missions, blood, and battle play over and over in their heads, and will not shut off no matter what. They believe that taking their own lives is the only way to shut it off.

The intent is to shut it off while they can still decipher real from unreal, to be to still see their family and friends as friendly forces, before it turns into live action, and before innocent Americans get hurt or killed.

Some Armed Forces People commit suicide because of the heaviness of it seeming unfair to them that their comrades were killed, and they were allowed to live.

There are many suicides that occur on missions and on battlefields in faraway countries. Often upon their return to the Homeland, they realize that they are now strangers among strangers, even amidst family and friends. It's done because of the way they were treated-which only made them afraid, insecure, and alone.

They feel unwanted, and that it is best to leave everyone uninterrupted and as they are.

So, they sign up for another combat mission, re-enlist, or recommission to go back to the now security of the familiars of war and friendship of the certainty of enemies.

It then becomes an honorable thing to be killed by a worthy enemy as opposed to being driven to death or to be killed by family, friends, or by homeland Forces.

Then there are those of the Armed Forces who have become solely conditioned to defend our Country against any enemy, anytime, anyplace, and for any reason.

During all the absence, rejection, hostile attacks, and abandonment by family and friends, and in many cases, by our Government too, they evolve into full time war machines. It becomes their every thought, and where they are most confident and respected, even by foreign enemies. This is now their only way of life. Without it, life is over for them.

Understand, there are many family members and friends who are genuinely intimidated and fearful of their Armed Forces service family member because they do not recognize them, and don't understand them. Because of that, they often don't care for them at all.

Spouses, fiancés, lovers, and often offspring quickly grow tired and weary of the physically and mentally wounded troops in their lives. So, they cheat on them, treat them harshly, steal from them, and waste their resources. They neglect them and often wish them dead.

My Personal Story

My "strangers among strangers" experience started while I was still on active duty. Even though I had advanced to a place where my family was able to live in the best and newest housing, my son was able to go to the best schools, and able to live in one the safest community in the greatest nation in the world, I still found myself faced with the "strangers among strangers" scenario.

I was in a unit, that was in the middle of a unit, that was within the middle of another unit. I wanted to be the best for my family and for my Country.

I excelled at all that I did for my family and my Country. I, like many other U.S. Armed Forces Service People, was, and probably still am, very good at things the average person should never be good at. However, each mission brought with it a deeper sense of pride, accomplishment, and secrecy. It also brought along with more and more chaos and division in my household. Mainly because each day, I was becoming more and more someone that my first wife did not recognize; despite me doing my duty and having provided for us the best housing, best neighbors, neighborhood, best friends, being financially sound , and having unlimited resources.

My being away on duty and missions created great voids between me and my family. Largely because when I would have to leave, rarely could I tell my wife where I was going, how long I'd be gone, or even when I'd return. Most of my answers were repeatedly that I was going on a mission. Period.

That was all that I was allowed to tell her at that time. At times, that's all I knew because we received as-needed instructions as we arrived at certain check points.

At the time, I could not understand why she could not just accept that I was on a mission on behalf of our Country and see that it was a good and honorable thing. Just as I was changing, she also was changing into someone I did not know. Though then, I chose to believe she was still the same; mainly because I could not afford to lose my focus from my Military duties, which was to me, my life and hers.

She started accusing me of being with and having other women that were someplace else during those times I was on missions. She was obsessed with that idea.

This was despite me returning home early a little over a year before that to surprise her, though it was me who got the surprise of my life . She and a guy, who used to be one of my best friends, sat in the living room naked with robes draped over them.
I was very proud that my military training had conditioned me to restrain myself. You see, I was still on a mission. I had only taken a break in my mission, hoping to make her happy with a surprising few hours

visit. Then, it would be back to my mission. It was the first and only time I left and took a break when my men couldn't take one too.

Shortly after that, she was pregnant. At that point, I had not touched her since some time before the night that my surprise to her turned out to be the worse surprise of my life.

I could not lose focus. I always had to remain mentally and physically mission ready. So, I made a quick decision that I was going to be this baby's father, and not let him be fatherless. This was regardless to who the biological father was. The thought of divorce had never occurred to me since I had never even heard of divorce.

I promised to never bring it up again, and she promised me the same. Plus, there was the fact that I could not afford for anyone to know that my wife had been with another man, or that I did not have control over my household. I especially couldn't let my men and superiors know, as well as my family.

That would have caused, both my men and my superiors, to lose their respect for me and their confidence in my abilities. I maintained my status and continued to excel in the military. I forged more and more provisions for my family's future, but only to come under more and more attacks by my then wife as she became more and more obsessed and abusive.

Her charge was that I was obsessed and in love with the military and with other women. There was only her, my son, my men, and yes, my Country.

To me, my duties in the military helped keep my family and America safe, but she treated me as if me doing my duties was outright betrayal against her.

It didn't help at all that on many missions. I could not carry on me or with me anything that would lead to home. So that in case of capture, no U.S. enemies could gain information and use it to compromise me, future missions, and positions.

Even with me explaining that, it wasn't enough. So, I started leaving pictures in my wallet and keeping on my wedding ring, only to remove it all on base at the office. She quickly figured out what I was doing. She thought that I was with other women, and that I was ashamed of her and my son. This could not have been further from the truth.

She repeatedly returned to her thoughts that I loved the military more than them, and before I knew it, my son had grown to sing me the same song, too.

Shortly after that, I was away in a foreign country, and my unit was finally able to take some much needed and well-deserved R&R or rest and relaxation. This was something I rarely did since I was a part of multiple units and operations outside of my primary unit.

I, and a few others with additional skills and training, would disappear into another mission. These were missions that would address immediate threats to our National Security.

At that time, we had no immediate or intermediate mission, so I took R&R . I spent a little time with our guys as they enjoyed free time for calling home, playing cards, and the swimming pool. They went out into the village, watched tv, listened to music, wore civilian clothes, and drank free beer and wine to their hearts' content.

I did not drink, but I did hold on to a Coors for fellowship's sake and comradery with our men. I later checked the guards and then turned in for the night.

Then suddenly, when it seemed that everyone was either asleep or passed out, we were ambushed. North Korea had dug a tunnel right into the inside of our base's perimeter.

They did this with inside intelligence and with the help of foreign nationals. We had losses. I barely escaped with my life. I overpowered the intruders. I awoke just as he came down with his knife right above me.

I've been fighting and shooting in my sleep, and sometimes when I'm awake, almost every night since. Our attackers escaped that night, and from that night forward I was never unarmed. Having gained enough rank, I carried an M60, and laced myself with extra belts of live ammunition, along with a .45 Caliber, a Thompson, a few grenades, and two bayonets. They were my sleep mates from that night on.

I purchased live ammunition in a nearby village. We always carried blanks and had to wait for White House orders to issue live ammunition. It was done that way to avoid incident in foreign countries. From that day on, no one in vicinity of me was going to die waiting for a call to ok the issue of live ammunition.

My tolerance became shorter, and my skills and awareness became sharper. I trained my men harder than anyone else so that they would be able to answer to any situation and any call. I trained myself harder than my men. I trained them on each level, and at each discretionary unit.

I started having flash backs when someone would question my orders. Personally, I would not question the orders of my superiors. I began hearing voices in my head telling me to kill, along with a single set of cross hairs over their faces.

The next thing I knew, my people started being hurt and bruised, and no one would say what happened.

Then later, someone told me I had just beat someone. They said that I just stopped and stood up straight as though nothing had happened. They said that I then asked what happened to them. To this day, I do not remember those spaces in my life.

At first, I thought he was just lying because I was hard on him. I wanted assurance that whatever happened, that they would be combat-ready, and able to accomplish any mission without any loss of lives or limbs.

For should they lose a limb, they'd remain a fighting force for America until the mission was accomplished. I did not believe them about what was happening with me until it had happened numerous times. I only believed them after they began to cover for me on missions.

My men had gotten so accustomed to my blackouts that they could tell when it was about to happen and would team up and bound me until it passed. Headquarters would come around to congratulate me on our missions in which they had accomplished. My men would pretend to be me on the radio.

I was proud that I had trained them so well, but quickly became ashamed that they had been covering for me. Even though it was not every mission that they did that, it had already been one time too many.

I have always had a problem with trusting foreign nationals, and foreign allies ever since I met President Saddam Hussein. He was a Colonel at the time, but I followed my orders despite that.

I seemed to have recovered and moved quickly up the ladder in rank and position and went on to accept more of those missions in which you may or may not return home. These missions deployed to various parts of the world. They were the kind of missions that you were asked if you would accept.

For a while, I didn't have any flashbacks. I went on so many missions and operations on different levels that I started having trouble remembering my real name. Yet, I could remember all the legend names and characters that used.

I would have to look at my actual nametag on my regular uniform or pull out my wallet and look at my ID card when I was at home. No one caught it, nor did I tell anyone. I just thought I'd deal with that later. I had to remain focused for any mission and could not fail my Country.

Later, one of my men went AWOL (absent without official leave/authorized permission). After I tracked him down, we were on our way back to base, and he told me why he had gone AWOL. He told me that all he did was ask me why someone else couldn't do what I had ordered him to do.

Then he told me after that, I started smiling, and instantly attacked him without ever saying a word. He said that he ran because he thought I might have killed him. He said he then continued running because he didn't want to be put into the stockade (a name for U.S. Army/ Military prison) for disobeying direct orders and running away.

Some time after that, I was home and woke up and saw my wife with ice in a towel around her neck. She told me that she'd tried to shake me to wake me. When she did, she said that I grabbed her neck , and started choking her while I was still asleep. She told me that she was barely able to break free, and that I never even woke up. After that, I reported what was happening to me to my superiors.

My superiors sent me to a special re-debriefing (the act of doing again questions and evaluation to both collect intelligence/ data from mission/duty and to assure mental and physical fitness to return to duty or regular civilian life) and psychological evaluation. Military doctors said I had suffered a disassociation attack and only needed some R&R (rest and relaxation).

I was ordered to take two weeks off with free paid mandatory leave. I rode my bike and worked out every day. I designed a new camouflage transport system during those two weeks. I also got caught up-to-date on military regulations, deployment tactics, and combat readiness. That is all I could think about, and for the most part, I still do.

Shortly after returning to duty, I was promoted and positioned for my next two promotions. I already held a top-secret security clearance and was skilled in covert operations, and other skills which I cannot reveal.

I was placed in a First Sergeant's position, which only confirmed to my then wife that I loved the military more than her and our son. I tried explaining to her that keeping my duties first was what kept my family first, but that meant nothing to her.

I wanted her to be proud of me, but it seemed she never was. I now think that it was probably because I was never able to share with her what it was that I did and where I was during those times I would be away on missions.

I guess she never really knew what to be proud of me for. Plus, we were both young. She started drinking a lot, and hanging out with subordinate enlisted men's wives, and leaving our son with people that I didn't know.

I believe it was because she didn't know how to deal
with who I had become, and with what she didn't
know about me. She started being gone and having
hangovers. That effected my duties. I had to reduce
some of my duties to care for my wife and child. I was
fearful in questioning her and even talking to her
about what she was doing. I was afraid it might have
led up to me having a flashback and possibly hurting
or killing my family. I could not risk that.

So, I just let it go until one night I found her with
people at a nudist party. Though she was fully clothed,
she refused to come home with me. I had to leave
before I turned into what had happened to me in past
times.
She came home at four a.m. I made our son breakfast
and went to work. Later, I called her and told her she
needed to go spend some time with her mother
because her behavior was getting in the way of my
duties. She agreed, and I took her and our son to her
mother's home.

Later, she told me that she would not be returning,
and that I had to either choose my family or the
military. I did not want to lose my family, but not
serving my Country was not up for debate at that
time. Shortly after that, while on a state-side FTX (in
country Field Training Exercise), we had a General
from the White House visiting our position (operating
location). When the General questioned me of my
choice of weapons, I was told that I had a dissociative

PTSD (Post Traumatic Stress Disorder) episode, and that I had attacked him. I was also told that I was ordered to be detained, then flown in for a psychological evaluation. I was later allowed to return to the FTX (field training exercise) Headquarters location.

I was not charged by the General, and neither had I any idea of what had happened until I was told by some of my comrades.

Later, after we returned to base, that same General summonsed me and he told me what had taken place. He said that I was a valuable asset to the United States Army, and to the citizens of America. That was why no charges would be brought against me.

I also received a letter of appreciation from that General that day, along with a message of thanks from President Carter.

I started sending intermediate units on missions without me. I feared who I was, the extent of my capabilities, as well as my inability to understand and control what was happening to me.

By this time, I had forged support in high places, as well as the possibility of notable enemies in the lowest and darkest places on earth.

I was very good at training boys to become men, especially those who others deemed unfit for military duty. My superiors and their superiors began to send those kinds of boys to me, especially those who were children of high-ranking officers and politicians. I enjoyed turning what everyone else called losers into weapons of mass destruction.

At times, I'm haunted by what I may have done to those great men's lives, to the lives of their families. I'm haunted by what they might be going through or putting their families through due to the depth of their training and experiences.

Besides that, I was horrified at the mere thought of leaving active duty for fear of not knowing what to do for a living. I didn't know what I would put on a job application or resume for experience. All my higher education was geared toward me serving thirty years in the military. At the time, I couldn't see putting the experiences that I did have on any job application. It had gotten so that I was not afraid of anything except getting out of the military and going into civilian life. It seemed as if I didn't know anything else except military, and that I did not want to do anything else.

I was good at being a soldier and accomplishing missions that would help to safeguard my country, and that's all I really wanted to do.

Finally, I decided to get out with some medical benefits. This was after long periods of dealing with the tug of war in my head and with my wife threatening to divorce me and take from me everything I owned and had worked for. I was plagued by the fear of possibly having a flashback and killing innocent Americans. For those reasons, I did not trust myself fully, and to a slight degree, I still don't. However, it was a most difficult period for me. I immediately went to my hometown's employment office for help in finding a job, and I was immediately faced by oppositions and harsh waiting periods for people who served on active duty military.

I was sent to file for unemployment, and government assistance-none of which I wanted. I only wanted to earn my own way. It seemed as if everywhere I went to seek employment, I was being penalized for having served my country.

I was quickly made to feel like I was an enemy of the State (someone accused of crimes such as treason against their own country and government). To go along with that, I would often hear people say, "he's been in the military", "watch how he walks and talks", and "you know the military has made him crazy". They'd say, "watch out". I've overheard many of my family members say the same. They often talked about me as if I wasn't present with them.

Looking at help wanted ads and TV ads proclaiming to hire Vets first, I responded to many of the ads only to find it was all a gimmick. That was repeatedly damaging to my soul. It was like I went from doing everything right to not being able to do anything right. It was like I went from being a silent national hero to an open object of disappointment, penalty, and rejection.

I wasn't worried, though. I had some money saved, and had bought property, both locally and in other states, to sustain both me and my family in case of divorce, and in case I had to go underground to protect my family from old foes of duty.

You see, that was another reason I was distant from my family. I wanted to protect them from my and our country's foes. Though I knew none of my family and friends would ever understand that, I tried to cover all my bases and leave no trails to my family just in case.

Just as we track down U.S. enemies and get to their families, our enemies come to the U.S. and do the same thing. I've done my share of deeds on foreign and U.S. soil. Yet, I don't want it to ever be such a day that those things do come home to me or my family, but I won't fool myself into thinking that it can't happen.

Then came another morning, and I awoke to see my wife and son covered in bruises and scars. I rose immediately with only one thought: to kill whoever had done that to them right under my nose. Then, my wife said to me, "You did this to us".

She said I was tossing and turning in my sleep and repeatedly yelling out numbers and the word fire. She had tried touching me to wake me out of it. Our son ran and jumped on the bed, and I attacked them both. My heart just seemed to have fallen to the floor. I got dressed and drove myself to the Sherriff's Department to turn myself in so that I wouldn't kill the people that I loved.

I told them what happened and asked them to lock me up and not let me back out. I wanted everybody to be safe from me. They were trying to be understanding and told me I seemed alright.

I then drove myself to the nearest V.A. Hospital, and tried getting them to lock me up, but they only gave me psychiatric medicines. I ended up going back home.

I became afraid to fall asleep for fear of what danger could happen. Every time I'd go to sleep, movies in my head would turn on, like on the big screen, with showings of my missions and of all that had gone on and all I'd done. It was as though I was living it over and over again. It was as if it was really happening.

Soon after that, I began again to hear kill command voices in my head along with overwhelming headaches and an inner urge to kill.

In efforts to deal with that, I researched local troublemakers and terrorizers. I began to stalk them and push them around to provoke them into either killing me or giving me a justification to kill them. God let them see that I wasn't right in the head. They would all fall in submission. God was truly watching out for me and them.

I was not able to tell my wife and family what I was going through because I was so worried that it would only confirm their theories that I was indeed crazy.

It was a very long time before I could somewhat share some things with V.A. doctors, but that was mostly because they seemed and looked even more quaky than I thought I might have been.

I started staying away from home to avoid the risk of falling asleep, and then waking up sorry for what might have happened while I was asleep; especially at night, but that all only made matters at home even worse.

I was constantly bombarded by my wife with her theories of me being out with other women or sneaking out going on missions for the military, She would say that the military was my real wife, not her.

There were times that I wanted to tell her what I was dealing with, and that what I was doing was my way of keeping them safe and keeping other innocent people safe as well. I was never able tell her any of this until just a few years ago.

When I did tell her, I asked her forgiveness for who I'd became and for what I had put her through. Oddly in that same month, she died. I don't know for sure that she died or was killed because of my sharing the truth with her for the sake of peace.

Back then, I was so afraid I would lose control and kill innocent Americans that I decided to take my own life in order to save theirs. I thought that I would still be a good soldier even if no one ever understood what I'd done.

I was taught early on that soldiers like me make the hard sacrifices that others couldn't accomplish, and that sometimes, our only reward and satisfaction would be knowing that we had helped keep America safe. That was very fulfilling for me and for people like me. That was worth everything.

So, I placed one of my weapons to my skull and without hesitation, I pulled the trigger. Nothing happened. I did it again. Nothing happened. I opened my front door and pointed the gun to the sky and pulled the trigger. I fired a few rounds, and there were no problems with my weapon.

So, I sat down, put the weapon against my head again, and pulled the trigger. Nothing happened. I cleaned my weapon and put in fresh rounds with my name, rank, and serial number scored on them. I fired several rounds into the sky. Then again, I tried to take my life, and failed.

I asked God what His problem was, and why wouldn't He just let me die for the good of everybody else. I stayed angry with God for quite some time. On some days, I felt that I couldn't even get that right. It felt like God was punishing me.

One day, it seemed that things were so heavy on me to kill. I heard a simple voice that said, "Go into the woods." I grabbed my sniper's riffle and did just that. I saw a large frog on the bank of a creek and shot it.

It seemed once my mind consumed the feel of the kill, and the smell of ammo and blood, all the pressure was off me. The voices to kill were gone, and that explosion of the headache was gone also. I wasn't about to tell anybody about that.

From that day on, for a long time, I knew what to do for relief. I'd sneak into the woods and kill something small. Thinking that was better than the risk of killing a person or killing a large animal, I began to hunt and fish to keep things in check and not arouse anyone's attention.

Over the years. I've met a few other Veterans who had learned to do the same thing, though we had only told this to each other. Even though we each embraced one another's fellowship, we subliminally kept our distance as to avoid arousal of suspicions by others.

I landed a job with the post office and was so happy. Then after three days, they told me that they had received an alert from Washington that said that I could not keep the job because it dealt with the public. It meant that it could possibly trigger flashbacks and endanger innocent people.

So, the next day I got another job. I was doing well if I went into the woods when I needed to. I was evolving. I had gotten to a place that I could tell when it was going to happen before it happened. However, it happened more often in public places, such as when I'd try going out to eat or something.

Everything would be fine, then suddenly, I'd see the walls turn bloody and other people would start looking like enemy combatants and terrorist targets. I would know that it wasn't reality, and that it was only in my head.

For everyone's safety, I would leave immediately and go into the woods and find some creature to sacrifice.

Afterwards, I felt bad for the animal, but it felt so good that I didn't kill any people.

When I would return home, my wife would be so mad and embarrassed about the way that I had to leave the outing. I would just let her fuss. I was both happy inside and sorry that I could not tell her what was going on with me all at the same time.

Later, I started an auto mechanic business. One day, someone from the V. A. came and told me that I could not have that type of business because it exceeded the decimals of noise level for my hearing loss and could cause further damage. I told him that I was no longer in the military. He then said, "Maybe nobody told you, but you are government property, and will remain so for the rest of your life." He went on to say that I was subject to be called back to duty without notice. He then gave me a paper with an appointment to begin work the next day in another government position.

It started out as one thing, but before I knew it, I was doing what I was good at again, and getting to serve my country. I felt the satisfaction of accomplishment that no high could compare to. And my reward? I could look around and see American people safe in the Homeland knowing that I had something to do with it.

It amazed me how people around would be oblivious to the goings on of the world and of the sacrifice made by the men and women of the Armed Forces, CIA, and other government agencies to keep them safe. That was the whole point.

My finances were solid again and I was in control of myself, my missions, and my personal life. I was no longer having flashbacks. I was still dealing with my wife's drinking, staying out, and accusing me of putting the government and other women before her.

I came home one day to find that she had moved out and had taken with her everything I had except the empty house. She destroyed anything else that she couldn't take with her.

She had maxed out all of our credit cards and emptied our bank account. She took her car and my car, a 1976 Road Runner which she always hated, along with all my parents', grandparents', great grandparents' and siblings' photos. She never cared for them.

However, I did maintain a few small armories of weapons, ammo, and chemical warfare gear to protect my family in the event my past missions ever came to my door step, or in case I became a target of corrupt political officials who had engaged U.S. Armed Forces in their personal greed missions that had nothing at all to do with National security.

When I went to divorce court, I was ordered to pay more than half my pay in alimony, child support, health insurance, car payments, and car insurance. That totaled about 75% of my pay along with awarding her all the money and property I had put aside so we both could live well together or apart. I was a Stranger among Strangers.

As if that wasn't enough knives in my heart, on the way out of the court room, she told me that she would make me pay for my son. She also said that I wasn't his father.

She continually reminded me of that every time I saw her. I found myself as a stranger among strangers, even though I had yet to realize it. I continued to try to keep it together. It was a struggle because most of my income went to my ex-wife.

I continued to secretly kill small animals when I would get headaches and flashes of missions. That was the only thing that made it all stop.

I still did my job well and appeared normal to others because I was conditioned to complete what I was doing. I could do two or three times the work load of most in about a quarter of the time. It was easy for me to be ahead in work and sneak away to get a fix. Along with that, I was afraid to sleep because of what could happen and because of the ongoing nightmares. I felt there was no one in the world with whom I could share what I was going through. I became ashamed for people to know I was military because of the way people treated Vets, and because I didn't want to risk anyone asking me what I did in the military. In time's past, when someone had asked me, and I told them the truth, they behaved as if I was the most awful person they'd ever seen.

I quickly learned to be secretly proud that I served. There is a lot more, but perhaps another time, or in another volume.

Later, I started college, and was in my prep courses of law, political science, an introduction to law. One night, a police car followed me from the campus parking lot to a dark area where there were no street lights. They then turned on their police lights, and I pulled over. Two police officers with guns drawn yelled, "Get out of the car, boy!" I asked, 'What am I being pulled over for? Do you want my driver license?"

Again, with guns still drawn, they yelled, "Get out of the car, boy!" I said, 'No, I know my rights, and I have the right to know why you followed me to a dark area and pulled me over."

They then yelled to me, "You are a dog, boy, and a dog don't have no rights." So, as to not make matters worse, I slowly got out of my car. I was doing all that I could to keep myself together so we all could go home safe. It was clear that they had no idea what they could possibly unleash.

As soon as I stepped out of my car, they started beating me with their clubs. I remember smiling and seeing only their faces in cross hairs. Then the next thing I knew, those two cops were on the pavement bruised up with me holding them down. They were begging me to release them.

I didn't know what to do, and I still don't remember what happened between that time. So, I told them I'd release them if they promised to not beat me again. They agreed. They got up and told me that they needed to take me to the station. I agreed to let them handcuff me thinking they'd keep their word. The moment they locked those cuffs on me, they beat me to the ground. Then, they dragged me on the pavement until they tore the skin from my knees.

My clothes were bloody. They threw me in the back of their patrol car and drove me around for about an hour at high speed. They repeatedly slammed on the brakes, causing me to slam into the metal partition in the car.
Finally, they took me to the police station where I requested to speak to the sergeant in charge to file a brutality complaint. The sergeant came with a clipboard in hand and a look of concern as he asked me to tell him what happened. He said that he could see that my rights had been violated. Then after

seeming to cling on my every word, he kicked me square in my groin. Then he had two men to drag me handcuffed to a far part of the city's jail where no one else was. I received no phone call, no food, and no medical attention the night I was pulled over.

I used my military training to stay fit and fed off my mind and from my own body. After three days, a man was mopping the jail hall floor, and I asked him to call my folks because no one knew where I was. He said that he couldn't because he didn't believe I was denied my call; however, he got word to my folks about where I was.

My grandparents and my brother, Ronald, came to get me. They could not find any charges against me, so they charged me the cost of replacing the damaged police uniforms and radios from the struggle. However, when I got my car from impound, they had ransacked it and most of my weapons and ammunition had been removed from it. None of it was turned in. I was unable to report them since they were illegal, special-made weapons and ammunition from overseas that I had smuggled here. My car was brand new. I had only had it for three days from special order. I was unable to drive that car again for thinking that those cops may be foreign operatives coming to retaliate for my past duties.

I struggled with telling myself that they were just a couple of ignorant cops. I had to coach myself from inner pressure, headaches, and a voice saying to kill them, and that they were threats to national security. I did not kill them because of their ignorance, yet I was not sure leaving them alive was the right thing to do had they been operatives.

I camped in the woods days at a time so that no one would be confronted by me and by what was going on with me. I made make-shift weapons and killed animals until the urges to kill the cops went away from me.

I felt bad for having to kill those animals, but at the same time, I felt heroic for having saved those men lives. I knew I'd never be able to explain that to anyone and make them understand. So, I didn't. I never thought that one day I would write about it.

When I returned to my grandparents' house days later, they asked where I had been, and told me that I had everyone worried. I told them I went for a walk and lost track of time. They started telling one another that the military had made me crazy as though I wasn't even there.

If only they had known that I had actually spent three days saving someone's life. Killing had never been a question, nor being killed, but not wanting to kill innocent people, even those who didn't understand the dangers of their actions.

Both what I've done in the name of National Security, and how ruthless, fearful, and misguided Americans have treated me have caused me to wholeheartedly trust no one. The effort I put into treatment for flashbacks and the medication from the V.A. have destroyed my reproductive organs and rendered me permanently impotent. I tell myself that was the cost of helping to keep America safe.

Then one day, it all took a toll on me. I started passing out, so, I went to the doctor. He said that I had developed a bad case of high blood pressure, and gave me more pills and said to me, "Don't drink any dark wine with this medicine. It could cause a heart attack." And what did I do? On my way home, I stopped and bought dark wine. In my mind, that doctor had just given me a way to end the nightmares that lasted through each night and over into idle moments of the day.

I had moved back into my house, had a 1.7-million-dollar insurance policy, and a will to take care of my family for life.
Then, a woman came to my house. She was a prostitute who I had helped several times to be a good mother to her kids, and not have to sell her body to strangers and family members for food and money.

I had never thought of sleeping with her. Even though my wife had divorced me, she was still the only woman I thought of in that way. I had helped her because seeing her sell her body, and being a mother, made it seem that the horrible things I'd done for a better life in the Homeland had not been enough.

She saw me on the floor through my window, broke in, and called the ambulance. When I came to, the emergency room doctor said that I was choking on my own vomit and at risk of having a heart attack. He said that I would have been dead had she not came when she did. In my mind, I thought, 'Oh, thanks for making me have to continue living like this. Ending my life was my whole plan.'

The woman claimed to have lost her home and needed a place to stay. The doctor did not want to release me unless someone would be home with me. So, I agreed to let her stay a few days. She started out being kind, and she seemed to be broken like me. I had not been treated with kindness like that in a while.

Weeks passed, and I didn't sleep for fear of hurting them while I was asleep. She asked me why I didn't sleep, and I told her then and there. She asked me to lay my head on her. So, I did. She rubbed my head, and I fell asleep there for about 12 hours. She said that she was afraid to move after what I'd shared with her.

Something didn't feel right. Then, one of her kids told me that every time I left for work, their dad would come by while he was drunk and spend the night with their mom. So, I left work early the next day and arrived home just as her ex-husband was getting in his truck and pulling away.

I just decided to leave. While I was packing, she called the police and told them that I had attacked her and was removing her things from my house. I advised them to not touch me and showed them my PTSD card that said they could not arrest me. They could only call the Department of Defense phone number on my card. Then, her oldest child came forth and told the police that his mother was lying on me about everything. Afterwards, they held her until I got my things and left.

Then some eight months later, she came to my job saying that she was pregnant by me. I could not see how that was possible, and I refused to believe it unless I heard it from her doctor. So, I went with her for a doctor's visit a few days later, then was told by her doctor that he needed my blood to confirm that the child was mine.

He came back and told us that it was, and I believed him without further question. I guess I just wanted my own biological child so badly that I wanted to believe it.

Also, I could not bear the thought of another child growing up fatherless. So, I married her. Later, I found it was all a con. Her doctor also a fraud. Now, I was married to her.

She wanted me to go to church so that Jesus could help me free my mind. So, I went to a nearby church and when it was the time to go forth to give your life to Jesus, I went forth. The preacher told me that all I needed to do was confess my sins, and God would forgive me, and I'd be made free. I asked if I could first speak with him in private, and he allowed it. When I confessed the summary of my sins to him, he told me that with what I had done, God didn't want me and that the devil wouldn't have me either. I wasn't at all surprised.

That made me determined to seek God's help for myself. This was after many years of feeling God had abandoned me and all like me. I went to my home church, and again I was told I needed to confess my sins and accept Jesus to be saved.

I started to remember that my grandmother would always tell me from a child that I would be a preacher one day. Then, both she and the Elder there, told me that after what I had done in service to my country that I could join the church, but that I'd never be saved, I'd never be anything in the church, and I would never hold any position in the church. Talk about Strangers among Strangers!

I accepted that at that time, because after all, I thought that they were the people who knew God and Jesus, not me. I accepted then that God wanted nothing to do with me. So, I just thought of myself on active duty. It was just my place to serve, do good, look out for others, and never expect any reward, or acknowledgement for it. I was cool with that since that seemed to be who I was.

However, I started studying the Bible anyway just to learn what would have been of me. Then, I stopped having flashbacks and nightmares. Instead, I started dreaming every night that I was preaching and having unction to preach. I would always dismiss it as only bad dreams and foolish thoughts. The unction to preach overwhelmed me one day at church and I found my mouth involuntarily confessing, 'I've been called to preach God's Word', and 'Here I am. Send me. I'll go.'
One month later, I had a heart attack, and the people that I knew were after my worldly goods acted as if I was already deceased. Their behavior ignited within me a pain that made a heart attack seem like nothing. When it seemed that I would recover and live and not die, and that no one would be getting anything, my new wife and other family and friends all left me while I was still in intensive care. Only my grandmother, Lucille P Drake, seemed to remain with compassion and support for me. Unable to return to duty, and unable to pay my bills, I lost my house, and had no home.

People would come by my hospital room and talk of things I used to own and of what happened to it all.

My grandmother asked me to come and go home with her and reminded me that I would always have a home with her.

I did go home with her to my old room, but it was not an easy thing for me I was used to being independent and not letting anything stop me. I recovered and got my own house again. I wasn't completely well, but well on my way. A cousin, who already owed me money and who had totaled my brand-new GMC truck, would come by my home each day and steal from me. Finally, I told him to not return because I was tired of him stealing from me and not to paying me while I was still sick. Yet, the next day he returned anyway bringing with him a friend of his. When they arrived, I was already outside chopping fire wood for my fireplace.

I remember pleading with him to leave. He and his friend were laughing. I started seeing only his face in cross hairs of the scope in my head. The next thing I knew, I was standing up laughing with a wood splitting maul in my hand looking down at a pile of rubble that was my cousin's car with him and his friend still trapped inside it.

I didn't know what had happened, and I still really don't, but it seemed obvious that I had had a flashback and nearly killed them both. When I realized what probably happened, I quickly pried them free from the wreckage. They both were fearful in coming out of the car until I walked away. Then, they both ran away as fast as they could.

My father, who worked for the Sherriff's Department, came to arrest me. I truly didn't know what happened, but that didn't stop everyone from asking me, and telling me what they think happened. I didn't know how to tell anyone what had happened to me, and nor was anyone interested in knowing. I was indeed a Stranger among Strangers.

My then wife returned, time and time again, and I felt I had to forgive her and take her back because of what I had done in my duty. That, in my mind, was worse than what she had done.
While she was gone again, I was called to duty, and seemed to be almost immediately one hundred percent fit for duty. I was treated with such dignity and respect and felt so welcomed by the U.S. military. I was gone for three months, and when I returned, it seemed that no one in my entire family had missed me at all. I was indeed a Stranger among Strangers.

However, I was well and financially sound again. All my bills were paid up, and I had extra bonus money. Of course, my then wife returned, and if I would refuse to let her in, she'd break in. She often called the police and lied saying that she feared for her life.

The police quickly saw that she was lying. She would run off and come back like that for ten years. I told her that I was tired of her. I was also unable to provide her sexual needs and wanted her to go and be with whomever she chose. I just wanted her to leave me alone.

One day shortly after that, she cooked me a special make-up meal with all of my favorite dishes. It wasn't until I had finished eating that I realized that no one else was eating. I then passed out. Twenty-four hours later, I woke up still on the kitchen floor, but I felt great and strong. She looked surprised and asked me did I feel sick. I told her no.

Later when I went to the medicine cabinet to take my meds, they were all gone. I ask her where they were, and she said that I had eaten all of them in my dinner the day before. She meant to kill me by overdosing me with food laced with my entire supply of medication.

I got better and better instead of it killing me. I knew then for sure that God had forgiven me and was on my side. Since I didn't see cross hairs and hear "kill", I felt as if God had also healed me.

She started threatening that if I tried to divorce her, or leave her, that she would lie and convince people that I was having sex with her child. The child that I basically raised and provided for by myself while she'd run off leaving her child with me. It felt like that could happen, so I would let her come and go until her daughter graduated.

We then moved to Cleveland, Ohio. After buying a house in an all-white suburban community, I was constantly assaulted and insulted by domestic workers, along with one poor fool, but not by the majority of the white community there.

She continued to come and go. I preached more and more and got better and better. As time went on, I bought a house for me to move in to be away from her. Then one day, her and her ex-husband went to child support court and to a hotel afterward. On her way home from the hotel, she got into a car accident which left her in critical condition. She suffered many broken and pulverized bones.

That was my perfect opportunity to be free from her, but I worried about what the church people would think of me leaving her in intensive care. I was unable to get any of her family or her children to come and be with her and be her caretaker. No one would help. So, I stayed and paid all her medical expenses, and took care of her until she recovered. She asked if she could move in with me in my new place that I purchased, and if we could give our marriage another chance. She asked me to forgive her for all her wrongs against me, and I did. Then after a day or two, I gave her a key. The next day while I worked in the basement, I heard the Cleveland Police call out, "Come out with your hands up!" They said that my wife Debra had called them and told them that I had beaten her and locked her out of the home. She told them that I had a gun and threatened to kill her.

They were already inside my home, so I asked them how did they get into my house? They answered, "Your wife unlocked the door and let us in." I replied, 'So, if she's locked out, how did she let you in?' I then told them that I was in the basement working, and that I did not own a gun. I had grown to hate guns, and Debra knew that. I refused to come up, but I welcomed them to come down into the basement where I was. I told them that I wasn't coming up there so that they could shoot me first and ask questions later.

With guns drawn, they came down into the basement where I was. Upon seeing me face-to-face, they holstered their weapons. They asked me if they could look around without a warrant. I welcomed them to do so.
 After searching my basement and house, they said that they were sorry, and asked what I wanted to happen there next. I told them I just wanted to be left alone by Debra permanently. They went out, then

came back in and told me that she wanted the furniture. I told them that I had just bought the furniture and had already given her all the furniture from the previous home. I told them that if that was what it would take for her to go away and leave me alone, she could take it all.

I asked them to wait until I hired someone to move all my new furniture and appliances to where she lived so there would be no further incident. I realized that she meant for me to be shot and killed by police that day.

A week later, she asked for my help to relocate to Mississippi. I was so glad for her to be as far away from me as possible that I said yes. Not only did I help, I paid for the full expense of her move.

Some months later, I hired attorney, Dean Calovas, to handle my divorce from her. What a very poor job he did! The next thing I knew, I was getting restrained from my house under the illusion that it was where Debra lived, and not me. I thought there must be some mistake because I lived there alone. Debra had never resided there at all. So, I removed the notice from the door and went into my home. Shortly afterwards, police came and arrested me for breaking and entering my own home. Debra had filed a restraining order claiming that was where she lived and that I lived in Mississippi.

After I was arrested by police, Debra then broke into and moved herself into my home. Then after moving into my home, and after I had made bail, she staged an emergency call soliciting my help. She said that she had fallen and could not get up and could not get any of her family to come and help her up. Remembering how her family had turned their backs on her when she was in serious condition from the car accident, like a fool, I rushed to her rescue. When I arrived, she was naked and trying to force herself on me sexually. After I escaped from her, she filed rape charges against me knowing full well that I lacked both the heart and the capability to do such a thing as that.

Because I was a Veteran, and was not intimidated easily, no one cared. My own attorney threatened to expose my impotency, that I was dangerous, and that I suffered with PTSD. He told me that I didn't want that because then, the whole world would know that I was impotent and had no manhood. From that point on, a new nightmare arose, and old ones restarted.
Then, on September 11th, 2001, commonly referred to as 9/11, the United States suffered attacks here on her own soil. When that happened, it reignited my alertness and distrust. To this day, it continues. I've only learned more ways to cope.

Conclusion

I often feel like a hypocrite while preaching, but at the same time, preaching is the primary thing that gives me relief and sanity.

I suffer from extreme paranoia. I don't like for people to touch me, and I don't like to touch people. I am very uncomfortable with anyone being aware that I am that way. I can hardly eat outside my home without becoming sick and vomiting it up. However, I am somewhat comfortable in the company of most other Veterans, but not all.

Nearly everything and everyone reminds me of missions I've been on, and of lives that have been taken. I am suspicious of almost everyone, yet I feel the need to protect everyone. I'm constantly on alert for terrorists and terrorist attacks in everything and in everyone I see and hear, as I am not in any way quick to touch things or people.

I feel obligated to protect Americans, and I just can't turn it off, though it seems that many Americans have tried to destroy me, and other people like me. Violence and shootings throughout our community and throughout our nation is torture to my soul. In it, I see lives taken and missions that I've been on with the purpose of keeping peace in the Homeland, yet these cruelties against Country-persons send out alarms that for far too many Americans, there is no peace.

That turns great things that I, along with other Armed Forces Service men and women like me, have done to protect our country and preserve peace in our Homeland seem like a waste of time, a waste of life, and a waste of ourselves. This reality adds to a heavy weight that so many of us carry.

Whenever I hear the sound of shooting of any kind, my mind then instantly identify what caliber of weapon. Along with that, I can smell blood and smoke of gun fire from great distances.

I do everything I can to be at peace with all, because in the absence of peace, there comes an overwhelming pressure to eliminate the threat, whoever they may be. Each time I master the pressure, I feel like a champion who has saved a life, instead of taking it. At times, the work necessary for me to master that pressure feels as if it will nearly kill me.

The nightmares are no longer a sporadic occurrence. They have become a constant part of me each day and each night. Even though most times I do feel forgiven, I still cannot bear the thought of having to kill anything or anyone anymore. Yet, I feel more than certain that I will in defense of family and country. I have not liked weapons for a long time now. Yet, I feel constantly and instinctively connected to them. I make it a point to never look at weapons. When I do, flashes of battles and perceived threats go through my mind.

When in doubt, I just stay home to avoid putting innocent American lives at risk.

This thing that I live with, and that lives with me, is not something anyone can simply turned on and off at will. So, I avoid all conflicts at all cost. This decision has cost me so greatly already.

Nevertheless, each day that I live without an additional body count to my charge is another day that I am proud to have helped save the day.

Constantly, I advocate for Americans at risk, and against those who bully and oppress them. It's like I have a need to maintain my oath to our country on a constant level, even when people are ungrateful. I remember to only accomplish the mission. Even if I am wounded, I cannot die until the mission is accomplished. I know that the only reward or acknowledgement I may ever receive is just knowing I helped save the day for Americans. I've tried stopping, but I can't. I guess for me there is not much that is more rewarding than that.

I know some people may feel sorrowful for me for that, but I feel sorrow for them because they will never know what keeping America safe feels like. I certainly hope that my story will shed some light for U.S. Armed Forces Active Duty and Veterans, their families, and friends to include everyone else.

Made in the USA
Middletown, DE
04 October 2022

11876423R10046